THE PRECIOUS PEARL

The Precious Pearl

The Story of Saint Rita of Cascia

Michael Di Gregorio, OSA

ST PAULS

Alba
House

Library of Congress Cataloging-in-Publication Data

Di Gregorio, Michael.
   The precious pearl: the story of Saint Rita of Cascia /
Michael Di Gregorio.
     p. cm.
Includes bibliographical references.
ISBN 0-8189-0940-4 (alk. paper)
1. Rita, of Cascia, Saint, 1381?-1457. 2. Christian saints—
Italy—Cascia—Biography. 3. Cascia (Italy)—Biography.
I. Title.

BX4700.R5 .D5 2002
282'.092—dc21
[B]

2002027399

Produced and designed in the United States of America
by the Fathers and Brothers of the Society of St. Paul,
2187 Victory Boulevard, Staten Island, New York 10314-6603,
as part of their communications apostolate.

ISBN: 0-8189-0940-4

Printing Information:

Current Printing - first digit   2 3 4 5 6 7 8 9 10

Year of Current Printing - first year shown
       2005 2006 2007 2008 2009 2010 2011 2012

Table of Contents

1. The Story

2. Legends

3. Disciple and Patron

4. Devotion and Devotions

1
The Story

A Treasured Gift

The closing years of the 14th century in Italy were filled with their share of hardship and struggle for secular and religious society alike. The cry of "vendetta" or "revenge" was the popular solution to many of life's challenges and conflicts. While the laws that monitored people's behavior could be strict and exacting, duty to family placed heavy demands on many shoulders, drawing some to risk the punishment of exile and even death, for the sake of honor. Within the Church the trials and human frailties of some who occupied positions of leadership often had a damaging influence on the unity and fidelity of great numbers of the faithful, resulting in laxity, division and even schism. In such a world the need for courageous men and women was very great. Fortunately, they were not lacking.

Antonio and Amata Lotti[1] were two such souls. Natives of Roccaporena, a tiny village belonging to the Republic of Cascia situated high in the Umbrian hills, they were so respected by their fellow citizens as to be given the difficult but im-

---

[1] Antonio Lotti's name is found in documents from the Convent of Saint Mary Magdalene in Cascia. His wife's name is given by tradition as Amata Ferri.

portant position of peacemakers for their town. Their selection for this duty indicates that they were well regarded by their neighbors for their integrity and generosity of spirit. Whenever conflict would arise between individuals or families, the Lottis would set out to bring the parties together, promote dialogue, and seek a resolution to the dispute. As devout Catholics, whose lives were well formed on the Gospel message of forgiveness and reconciliation, they received the blessings promised to those who sow the seeds of peace.

Foremost among those blessings, in their estimation, was the birth of their only child in the year 1381. Antonio and Amata had been married many years and had almost given up hope that their long and fervent prayers for a child would be favorably heard. When it seemed time to resign themselves to God's denial of their petition, Amata finally conceived and, in the course of time, joyfully presented her husband with a baby girl. Overwhelmed by God's gracious favor to them, they looked upon their daughter as a precious jewel and appropriately gave her the name Margherita, which, in the Italian of the time, signified "pearl." From the day of her birth until today, however, she has always been known by the affectionate diminutive, "Rita." According to custom she would have been baptized almost immediately, but not in

Roccaporena, which was not a big enough place then to have a parish priest of its own. Rather, she was carried to the Church of Saint Augustine, which sat high on the hill of Cascia, overlooking the city whose name would be forever linked to hers in history.

One of the treasured stories concerning Rita which has been passed down through the centuries — and there are many of them — belongs to the months not long after her birth. Antonio and Amata were out one day tilling the fields and left Rita sleeping in a cradle in the shade, close enough so they could observe her movements and hear her cries. Another laborer working the ground with the Lottis cut his hand and, running back to the nearby house for some bandages to stop the bleeding, was startled to see a swarm of bees circling little Rita's face, even entering and exiting her mouth. Though Rita's sleep was not disturbed in the least, the man instinctively began to wave away the bees with his hand — his injured hand. When the bees had left and he was satisfied that Rita had not been harmed, he suddenly realized that the bleeding of his hand had stopped and that his wound was healed!

The routine of daily life in Roccaporena was largely predictable. Births, marriages, funerals and feast days helped to bring some diversion to the normal cycle of events, but families who earned their livelihood from working the land and tending their flocks, as the Lottis did, found their days full of activity and their nightly rest well-earned. Even as a young girl Rita would have become a welcome helper to Amata in the household chores. We can imagine her walking to the nearby River Corno to do the wash on rocks worn smooth by generations of women and girls before her, or baking bread in the backyard oven, or shelling peas as she sat with her friends on stools in front of the house while greeting passersby along the road. When she was old enough her parents provided Rita with some schooling, probably through a tutor they had agreed to pay with their produce or baked goods. We know that Rita surely was taught to read and write, which could not have been said of many young girls, or boys for that matter, who would have been her companions.

On special days Rita loved to go to nearby Cascia, less than a mile's walk along the hill that winds its way beside the River Corno. Cascia had much to attract Rita's attention. While Roccaporena sat low in a valley surrounded by tall rocks and hills and was a relatively remote and quiet village, Cascia sat high on a mountainside and was filled with activity and excitement. Situated on a crossroad of commerce that ran from Naples in the south to Florence in the north, Cascia would have left Rita entranced by its sounds and movement, especially on market day, when everyone, it seemed, filled Saint Augustine's Square in the center of town.

Formed as she was by parents who were very devout in the practice of their faith, Rita learned early on to combine her enjoyment of amusements and activity with a similar delight for the things of the spirit. On these visits to Cascia she would not miss an opportunity to slip into Saint Augustine Church for a quiet moment of prayer, to attend Mass or, in time, to make her confession. She might talk with one of the friars who would fascinate her with stories of the saints who were especially venerated there: Saint Augustine of Hippo, the church's patron; Saint John the Baptist, patron of the small chapel that once stood on the same site; and Nicholas of Tolentino, a friar not yet canonized, but whose reputation for holiness was already widely known.

Often Rita would also visit the nearby Convent of Saint Mary Magdalene, which housed a community of Augustinian Nuns, one of whom was a relative of the Lottis. Rita came to know the sisters well, and they her. Over the years her admiration for these women and attraction to their way of life grew stronger and stronger, until Rita concluded that God was calling her to join them.

When she shared her feelings with the nuns they sent her home to speak about the matter with her parents.

A Safe Path

It is not difficult to imagine the excitement that filled the heart of Rita as she contemplated what life in the convent would mean for her. The weighty demands of daily life helped girls like Rita to reach a maturity of purpose and attitude quite early back then, such that even as a young adolescent she felt she could give herself wholeheartedly to God and find happiness just as she observed it in the lives of the sisters she came to admire. If there were one difficulty to her dream, it would be the thought of leaving her aging parents whom she held dearer than anyone or anything on earth, and who she believed, though happy with her choice, would no doubt also feel the pain of separation.

Rita's announcement to her mother and father was probably not unexpected. As attentive parents who knew well their daughter's natural goodness and fervent religious spirit, as well as her frequent visits to the Augustinian convent in Cascia, they may well have anticipated this piece of news. What a surprise and disappointment to

Rita, then, to hear them say that they could not support her choice of vocation. And what a burden for them to have to tell her so! They had foreseen the possibility of this day's arrival and were prepared to explain to Rita their reasons for asking her to forego her plans. Their reservations centered principally around two difficulties. The first was the climate of hostility and violence that permeated society. It was precisely their work as peacemakers that made Antonio and Amata so very aware of how easily the offenses people felt caused disruptions in society and pitted families against one another in longstanding and bitter enmity. How frequently anger turned to hatred, and hatred to violence, and violence to tragedy. Even religious life was not immune to the forces of evil that recourse to vengeance could inflict.

The Church, too, was experiencing great difficulties at this time that brought confusion and discouragement to many people. Only shortly before Rita's birth had Pope Gregory XI returned the papacy to Rome from its long exile of almost 70 years in France. The Avignon Captivity, as the period was known, was caused by extreme political pressure, which civil rulers exerted on the Church and its leaders. When Gregory died in 1378 some of the Cardinal electors were not pleased with his successor and set about electing a pope of their own choosing. Thus began a long and sorrowful period of schism in the Church which had far-reaching effects, even in distant Roccaporena. It simply did not seem to Antonio and Amata that conditions were suitable for Rita to embrace religious life. Instead, they told her of their own plans for her future.

The Lottis believed that married life would provide Rita with security and safety, and they had arranged a match according to the custom of the day. Their choice was a young man by the name of Paolo Mancini.[2] Paolo would have been a member of the same social class as the Lottis, probably himself a native of Roccaporena or Cascia, or at least of the surrounding area. In their desire to encompass Rita with the protection and security which neither society nor church could give her, they assuredly would have gone to lengths to insure Paolo's uprightness and integrity.[3]

As Rita listened to her parents' explanation,

---

[2] His Christian name is given variously as Paolo Ferdinando, or Paolo di Ferdinando. The family name, Mancini, however, is recorded in a notarized document of Saint Mary Magdalene Convent.

[3] Legend paints Paolo as a violent, even abusive, husband. Modern research has shown, however, that the basis for this tradition is the misreading of an ancient document, which intended to describe as "ferocious" Rita's forehead wound of a thorn, and not her husband. See the section on *Legends*.

she was able to appreciate both their concerns for her safety and their genuine desire for her well-being which, she knew, were born out of love. She understood, without question, that their interest was always for her good and she trusted the wisdom which experience had gained them. While disappointed at first that her plans would have to change, she was also confident that God's will for her was being expressed through Antonio's and Amata's good judgment. She accepted their decision and put the thoughts of convent life aside.

The young couple were married in 1395 when Rita was fourteen years of age. They did not immediately set up house together, however. While the law permitted formal marriage for a girl of Rita's age, the sealing of the marriage contract had to wait another two years. In the interim Rita continued to live at home with her parents, and Paolo with his family. Society looked upon them, nonetheless, as solemnly and permanently committed to each other. When the required time had passed, Paolo appeared at the Lotti door and escorted his young bride to the home he had prepared for them both and for their future family. Their dream and their prayer were to spend many happy years together there. Before very long Rita and her husband would be blessed with two sons. While their names are not known with certainty, tradition remembers them as Giangiacomo and Paolo Maria and sometimes describes them as twins.

The Mancini household was full of vitality and happiness. It could not have been otherwise, for its mother, the heart of the home, was already walking the path of holiness. She loved her husband and cherished her sons, and her own satisfaction was found by pouring her generosity and affection upon the three of them. She always maintained the conviction that this was, after all, God's plan for her, and it was this that helped her through the more difficult moments and challenges that life sometimes brought.

Hatred's Cruelty

Unlike Rita's parents, Paolo Mancini did not earn his livelihood off the land nor by tending flocks or caring for animals. He was employed, rather, as a watchman in one of the towers of the area known as Collegiacone, situated between Roccaporena and Cascia. As was sometimes the case, Paolo may have obtained this position by way of political appointment and, while it indicated some standing in the community, it may also have been a cause of the tension and irritability that sometimes characterized his behavior. By disposition he was somewhat quick-tempered and could rather easily be brought to anger. Rita, however, by her patient understanding and genuine goodness was able to smooth over even this rough edge to Paolo's personality. The one truly challenging difficulty that always hung over the family as a threat and sometimes erupted into open conflict, was a generations-old controversy that pitted the Mancinis against another local family. Rita's secret, daily prayer was that Paolo and their sons would never be directly touched by it.

Together husband and wife provided a solid home life for their two children, whom they sought to raise with the same values and ideals of Christian living that they themselves had received. The pressures of society can be weighty, however, and the Mancini home was not immune to their influence. Despite the noble heritage which Antonio and Amata had bequeathed as agents of peace and reconciliation to their daughter and her family, and notwithstanding Rita's own gentle and compassionate disposition, the widespread spirit of hostility and rivalry that characterized large segments of public life also played a significant part in the Mancini children's human formation. This influence was to reveal itself in a very dramatic and painful way when tragedy suddenly touched the lives of this otherwise peaceful and united family.

It was the year 1413, a day like any other. At first, Rita probably did not think it unusual that Paolo was late again in returning from work. His duties often required him to be flexible in the time he gave to his job. After all, public safety depended on men like Paolo who were on watch at the tower in turns throughout each day and night. On this particular day, however, Rita grew more preoccupied than usual by Paolo's delay. As the hours passed, her concern increased. Perhaps he had become ill or had injured himself, she thought. She dared not alarm her sons with these ideas, but appealed to some neighborhood men who accompanied her to the tower.

It was not a long walk to the tower of Collegiacone, but long enough to allow tension and anxiety to build within Rita as they approached. It was diffused, in an instant, however, as they caught sight of Paolo's body on the ground, the sign of his brutal murder clearly visible. How many perplexing thoughts raced through Rita's mind, how many conflicting emotions did she feel! She sensed immediately the cause of her beloved's cruel fate: that long and relentless feud that plagued his family. It had claimed another victim now! Another widow! Another fatherless family! How often this same story had been repeated! How many more would have to be touched by it? Would one of her own sons now take his father's place and someday suffer the same senseless end? Hardly had she time to feel her own pain of loss at Paolo's death when thoughts of their children stole her attention.

Rita was not only a practical woman she was a deeply faith-filled one as well. The only possible response to what hatred's cruelty had inflicted upon her now was the one she had learned as a child from her parents. They had so wanted to protect Rita from violence such as this but, of course, they could not. Nor could they have foreseen the irony of its eventual brutality, touching her in the very person they had hoped would be her defender and protector. Instead, their words and example of years past would have to offer her a way to deal with it all. But Rita also drew from her own personal religious convictions to meet the great challenge of Paolo's death with confidence in God and in the wisdom of the Gospel. Jesus' message of forgiveness was well known to her. Like every other Christian she had found many occasions to practice it in her life and to teach its importance to her children. Never before, however, had the reason for its application been so great or so personally challenging. Rita knew, all the same, that in things both great and small Jesus' word was the sure path to freedom and to peace. She did the only thing possible to her. She pledged to God her forgiveness of Paolo's killer.

The neighbors who had accompanied Rita to the tragic scene now carried Paolo's lifeless body home. Rita hurried before them to break the painful news to her sons herself. Along the way she carefully rehearsed her words, anxious to embrace them with the fullness of a mother's comfort and compassion, yet ready to discourage even the slightest indication of retaliation which, she suspected, might be their immediate response to her unwelcome news.

The Mancini boys were young teenagers now and their reaction to the report of their father's cruel death was not surprising: a jumble of shock, sadness, fear, confusion and anger filled them both. Rita understood well their feelings and their needs and sought to share with them the resources of her own deep spiritual life. It was her heartfelt prayer that these two sons of hers could experience the consolation and peace which faith in Christ and his teaching were already bringing her in the face of such an horrific offense.

Sorrow Tripled

A mother's love can be powerful and persuasive but, sadly, in this instance it was not sufficient to satisfy the sons of Paolo and Rita in their grief. Other forces were also at play, calling for their attention and allegiance. There was growing each day in Paolo Maria and Giangiacomo the certainty that society's expectation — shared forcefully by a number of their Mancini relatives — was that filial duty required them to avenge their father's murder. The honor of the family name demanded as much!

Rita, for her part, continued to speak the message of forgiveness, but her words increasingly struck her sons as feminine weakness rather than Christian virtue. While they never doubted the suffering and pain their mother experienced personally at their father's death, they saw their own very different way of dealing with the tragedy as the more just and necessary one. As the weeks and months passed they planned their scheme, careful not to discuss it openly lest Rita be doubly burdened by their determination. Motherly intuition, however, penetrated the silence they pretended, and led her to raise the issue repeatedly, hoping to change their hearts. The struggle was trying and intense, for Rita was in dispute not only with the attitude of her sons, but with the arguments and customs of a large segment of society that was urging them on. More than once she pointed to the image of Jesus hanging on the cross, asking them to recall his words of forgiveness toward those who had placed him there. Nothing of hers, however, seemed to reach them.

Convinced, at last, that pleading with them was useless, Rita redoubled her prayers to God, asking him to do what she, clearly, was unable to do, and bring her children to forsake their misguided path. Her fear was not only for the recurrence of violence in which they were intent to take part, but also for the loss of their innocence, indeed, of their very souls. Their father had, unquestionably, suffered a cruel and violent end, but he had not been responsible for another man's death. Far greater and crueler would be Rita's suffering now if his sons did what had been done to him.

One day, as Rita was absorbed in deep prayer on her sons' behalf, she became entirely certain — with a new and penetrating degree of awareness — that her desire for the welfare of Paolo Maria and Giangiacomo could not be greater than that of God himself, whose sons they also were. She, therefore, entrusted them completely to his wisdom and providence and, as she had done previously in her life, put aside her own plans.

A year had not fully passed since Paolo's death when tragedy once more entered the home of Rita Mancini. Though it was not the particular tragedy she had once feared, it was no less cruel and painful for Rita. Even as her sons continued to plan their means of retaliation against their father's assassin, the frailty of life became manifest in the form of a deadly illness which afflicted Roccaporena. Among its many victims were Paolo Maria and Giangiacomo Mancini. Cut down in their youth, it would fall to others to carry out their plan of retaliation.

Could Rita have ever imagined just how her prayer to God would be answered? Could she have foreseen the costly price of her sons' innocence? Somehow, she believed, he would make all things work to the good. She asked now only for the strength to accept his will. Life had changed so radically for Rita, and so quickly. At thirty-two years of age, she knew the great hardship of losing her husband and both of her children. Alone in the world, robbed of the three people she held most dear, Rita placed her trust in him who had suffered so much for her so that her present suffering would not be in vain.

The Second Calling

The small hamlet of Roccaporena is surrounded still today, as it was in Rita's time, by tall, rugged, rocky peaks that protect it from the threats of man and nature without. One of these heights, known as the *scoglio,* had long been a choice place of refuge for Rita, but especially so after the death of her children. Here she would spend many hours in prayer, bringing to God the questions common to anyone who had suffered Rita's misfortunes. Here she wrestled with her emotions, she poured out her heart in prayer, and sought the guidance to know God's designs for her. None of this was easy for Rita. Her loss was great; her pain was deep! But she was not one to allow it to absorb her energy or draw her into herself.

When she was not atop the *scoglio* Rita could often be seen at the local hostelry caring for strangers and travelers who had come to Roccaporena in search of hospitality. Here she found a rewarding way to spend her time and a vehicle to channel her warm and generous spirit for the good of others, as well. As the months passed, Rita developed a satisfying routine of prayer and work and, while this never filled the void which the loss of her loved ones left in her, she was very much at peace.

One day as she was engaged in prayerful recollection at her mountain retreat, Rita found her thoughts turning again and again to her childhood years and especially to the visits she had often made to the Augustinian Nuns in Cascia. Though as wife and mother those visits had become less frequent, she maintained contact with the sisters, nonetheless. They had been a great comfort to her after the death of Paolo and her children. Their life of prayer and total dedication to God once again became very appealing to her. Could it be possible, she wondered, that she might join the sisters now as she had once wanted to do? Though she had dismissed this idea years earlier, before her marriage to Paolo, and had never regretted that decision, she was now free of all family responsibilities and her attraction for a life of prayer and recollection had only grown stronger and stronger. It was an idea that required much thought and prayer, and Rita gave herself to both with earnestness.

The nuns at Saint Mary Magdalene were pleased to see Rita again. She had always been a welcome visitor to the convent and was admired by the entire community for her gentle and deeply religious spirit. Ever since the triple tragedy that touched her life, the esteem they felt for her increased all the more as they observed her steadfast serenity and resignation. The nuns showed interest in hearing how life was progressing for Rita and listened carefully as she told of the happiness she found in offering hospitality to Roccaporena's visitors. They were not prepared, however, to hear her reveal what she had come to believe was God's most recent invitation to her.

Rita was very frank with the nuns, explaining how she had considered this idea of a "second calling" for some time, bringing it to prayer repeatedly, before bringing it finally to them. The reaction of the Augustinians was mixed. Some were delighted — she was such a good person; while others were hesitant — she had been married for eighteen years and had borne two children! Rita would have understood their concerns, and the need, of course, for them to discuss her situation among themselves. When she returned to the convent sometime thereafter to receive their decision she was surprised and disappointed: they could not accept her.

Perhaps she had been mistaken. She might have misread the signs she felt were calling her to religious life. Once again Rita brought her questions to prayer. She spent even more time atop the *scoglio*, reviewing her considerations and asking God for some clear indication of his will. But no sign came other than a deep inner conviction that this indeed was what God wanted for her — and for the nuns themselves.

The nuns were taken aback by Rita's return to the convent a second time and her insistence that God wanted her to be part of their community. While they respected her sincerity, they simply did not agree with her conclusion and, sadly, had to repeat what they had said previously, this time, however, explaining the reason for their denial: the scourge of vendetta that had taken Rita's husband was too great a threat to the peace and stability of convent life. Of course, the nuns understood that Rita held no grudges, that she had forgiven Paolo's enemies, and had proclaimed forgiveness to her children as well. But they also knew that Rita had not prevailed, and that Paolo's relatives were still embroiled in rivalry and hostility with his assassin's family. Despite Rita's personal act of pardon, the pressure of society's expectations for revenge was too risky.

Now Rita found herself in a true dilemma. Was this second refusal of the nuns not a sure sign that what she thought to be God's call to her was, in fact, mistaken? Earlier in life she had no doubt that her parents were reliable indicators of God's will when they first dissuaded her from pursuing a religious vocation. Should she not accept the convent's decision as equally certain? But she could not. The more she tried to resign herself to the nuns' refusal, the more she felt the pull within summoning her to Saint Mary Magdalene. And it was clear that it was the Convent of Saint Mary Magdalene to which the Lord was calling her. The thought of approaching another of the several communities of women then existing in Cascia was simply not an option for her. Her prayer now became an urgent plea for God's encouragement to bring her back to the convent doors a third time.

It was only the conviction that she was following God's will and not her own that made it possible for Rita to repeat her request to the nuns for acceptance. She spoke with confidence which impressed them, but not even her sincerity and self-assurance could overcome their fear. This was the final refusal. They told her, ever so politely, that she should not ask them again.

It was no longer a question of seeking discernment or confirmation, but of finding an advocate to assist her and plead her cause. How could it be that God who was calling her to Cascia was not removing the obstacles that sought to keep her out? Or was this a test, God's way of strengthening her resolve and preparing her for the challenges that lay ahead? As she left the convent disappointed and frustrated by her ineffective pleading, she walked up Cascia's hill and stopped in the Church of Saint Augustine before returning home.

Three Faithful Friends

It was in the Church of Saint Augustine that Rita's Christian life had begun and there, too, that her

Christian spirit was often nourished during her many visits as a child. There she had made the acquaintance of the three giants of faith revered by the people of Cascia: John the Baptist, Augustine of Hippo and Nicholas of Tolentino. Frequently over the years she had looked to these three for inspiration and called upon the assistance of their prayers in her various needs. She came to invoke their aid now, confident that they would help her.

John the Baptist continued to be honored on the hill of Cascia many decades after the small church dedicated to his memory had given way to a much larger one named to honor Saint Augustine. And fittingly so! John, of course, was the great prophet who bridged the Old and New Testaments, announcing the imminent coming of the Messiah, and urging his own disciples to follow Jesus when at last he appeared. "No greater man has ever been born of woman," Jesus himself had said of John. And this greatness was due in no small part to the very humble role the Baptist was content to play once the Lamb of God had come. John's very identity and vocation in life are understood in relation to Jesus. He knew himself to be but a voice calling others to prepare the way for Jesus, the Word; he was a witness to the Light who would dispel the darkness of sin that John was urging his followers to renounce. From John Rita learned to whom she was to give her attention. From John she came to understand the value of pursuing and proclaiming the truth and the importance of God's will. Rita was ready to give her all for these goods just as John himself had done.

The second of Rita's patrons was Saint Augustine of Hippo, the spiritual father of the friars who built the great church on the hill in the early 13th century. When converted to the Catholic faith at age 32, Augustine renounced his former way of life and all of his worldly ambitions, including the possibility of marriage, in order to devote his entire life to God as a monk. He had been exposed to a life of Christian faith from childhood by his saintly mother Monica, but was early on driven by a great desire for wealth, fame, and career as well as by a strong passion for pleasure which he saw no reason to curb. Augustine was also a very talented man, whose ability as a teacher of public oratory and philosophy eventually won him a position in Milan where he was exposed to the preaching of the famous bishop, Ambrose, and was gradually drawn by him to the faith of his mother. Following his baptism at 33, Augustine returned to his hometown in North Africa, where he established his monastery and was resolved to spend the remainder of his life. On a visit to the city of Hippo, however, he was selected to become — to his great dismay — assistant priest to the then bishop whom he eventually succeeded as chief shepherd of the diocese. Even as bishop, however, Augustine continued to live the simple, common life of a monk, and wrote his *Rule* for those who wished to follow his example or live together with him. Bishop Augustine was an indefatigable teacher of the faith, a powerful preacher of the Word of God and a tireless servant of the Church. His many sermons and books display his deep spiritual convictions, rooted in the experience of his conversion years earlier, when he became powerfully aware of God's love for him and God's grace ever present to assist him. Rita would come to know, as Augustine did, how the sometimes seemingly absent God is at work even in the darkest, most disappointing experiences of life, inviting us to choose his will which is the sure path to our peace.

The third member of Rita's court of heavenly patrons was Nicholas of Tolentino, who was not yet a saint when Rita first came to know of him. He would become one during her lifetime, however, in circumstances that suggest his strong intercession on her behalf, as will be seen later. His canonization, 141 years after his death, would make him the first member of the Order of Saint Augustine to be so honored. Nicholas was born in 1245 in the town of Castel Sant'Angelo in the region known as the Marches of Italy near the Adriatic Coast. His birth was similar to that of Rita's in that it was also the answer to his parents' long and faithful prayers. They had had recourse to the intercession of Saint Nicholas of Bari to obtain a child, and had even made a pilgrimage to his shrine in that southern Italian city. Faithful to the promise they had made there, they named their firstborn after the saint and dedicated him to the Lord. As a young boy Nicholas was greatly influenced by the preaching of an Augustinian friar and requested admittance to the Order. He was accepted in 1259, received his training in various houses of the Augustinians, and was ordained a priest. The greater part of his life was spent at Tolentino, however, where he was engaged in sacramental ministry, especially the Sacrament of Penance, and tireless service to the sick and the poor, while pursuing a life of intense prayer and mortification. Nicholas had a warm and attractive personality and was known for his great patience and compassion toward the needy and afflicted. This aspect of his character and charity even extended beyond the grave to the souls of the faithful departed, as is demonstrated in a famous story. Once in a dream Nicholas was visited by a friar who had died only recently and begged for Masses to be offered for himself and for his companions who were suffering in purgatory. Nicholas told the prior of the community what he had experienced and was instructed to offer Mass for the next seven days for these individuals. He did so, and after the seventh Mass, was once again visited by the deceased friar who thanked him profusely that his prayers had gained him and many others entrance into heaven. Ever after Nicholas' reputation as a special advocate of the faithful departed became widely known and his intercession was continually sought for their freedom and eternal peace. Both before and after his death in 1305, very many miracles were attributed to the intercession of this good and holy friar, causing his confreres to recommend him to the faithful as a powerful advocate with God. Rita was one of the many who looked to him as a friend in prayer, but also as a reliable example of a soul attentive to the needs of the sick and the poor. At the death of her parents, husband, and children he also became for her a trustworthy advocate on their behalf.

A Mission of Peace

The months that had passed since Rita first approached the nuns of Cascia with her request seemed long and trying. It was difficult to reconcile the hard reality of their rejection with the certainty she had of God's will. If there was any consolation for Rita it was in the knowledge that she had done everything possible to be an agent of his designs. Or so she thought!

Rita's prayer now had become in large part a plea for patience and for the wisdom to know what more she might do. One evening, while deeply absorbed in reflection and supplication atop the *scoglio*, it suddenly became evident to Rita that she was not alone. Others had joined her there, interrupting her cherished moments of privacy. Turning, she noticed not intruders, but the familiar faces of her three heavenly patrons whose presence filled her with an extraordinary feeling of peace. They had come in answer to her prayers and would show her the way through the barred doors of the Cascia convent.

Her saints reassured Rita that the path she was attempting to follow was, indeed, the right one. She had acted wisely and selflessly and her prayers had been heard. Her heroic gesture of forgiveness and her brave efforts to foster the same in her sons had not been wasted. There was but one thing more to do. The gift of peace that she had always enjoyed, even in her darkest moments, now was to be shared with those who had always resisted peace the most. The gift she had received she was to give freely as gift. This was the key that would unlock the doors of Saint Mary Magdalene Convent and gain her entry.

Suddenly Rita was alone again. Had she been dreaming? Was her imagination getting the best of her? Perhaps she had been spending a little too much time on the *scoglio*. She wondered. There was no sign of anyone else's presence, only a strong conviction of what she must now do.

The following day Rita went to the home of Paolo's family. She was accustomed to stop by from time to time and so her visit did not surprise them. Almost four years had passed since Paolo's murder and three since the boys' deaths. Each knew the other's mind regarding the tragedy and the ongoing vendetta, and had long before stopped discussing these issues. There seemed no point to it. This day, however, Rita raised the topic again, but with renewed fervor.

She reminded the gathered family members that antipathy and stubbornness had for generations caused suffering and pain not only to their enemies but also to themselves and to those they loved most. It was shameful enough that their hostility was a sin against God, but it was a disgrace to the honor of the Mancini name as well. Finally, Rita spoke of her own personal suffering, prolonged and intensified now, by the refusal of the nuns to receive her on their account.

This was not a message that was new to the Mancinis, but this time it struck them with a powerful force they had not known before. They were deeply and genuinely moved and told Rita so, and promised that, for their part, they would put aside all claims to vengeance and be willing to make peace with their rivals, the assassins of Paolo. They then asked Rita to serve as mediator, conveying this pledge to their adversaries. Even Rita was taken aback by such a response. She realized that something more than her simple words had touched the Mancini hearts. And as she left, the names of John, Augustine and Nicholas were on her grateful lips.

Rita did not give much thought to the reception she would receive at the home of the Mancini's rivals. She knew only that she was on mission, not only for her own sake, but for the welfare of an entire people as well, just as her parents had been so frequently many years earlier. The family received her cordially; they had never had anything against Rita. Indeed, many of them felt great sympathy for her and admired her integrity and kindheartedness. They listened intently as she made her case and were astounded to receive the overture of peace that she brought from the Mancinis. They would consider it, they promised, and Rita departed.

Several days later Rita received her answer in a return visit with a request for her to arrange a meeting with the Mancinis. On the day appointed, the heads of the two families came together and, in the presence of Rita, exchanged a peace embrace affirming their commitment to put aside all forms of reprisal and hostility and to live ever after in friendship. A written agreement to this effect was signed and given to Rita, who happily brought it to the nuns. Sometime later a fresco depicting the scene of the peace embrace was placed on a wall of the Church of Saint Francis in Cascia,[4] an enduring reminder of the power of good over evil and a testament to the widow whose forgiving spirit achieved the impossible.

Embracing the New

Rita was thirty-six years old now. When she was finally able to bring the peace agreement to the Augustinians they were as delighted as she was at what had been accomplished, and welcomed her into their community. She had experienced so

---

[4] In the centuries since, the figures of the two men were covered over with another painting, but the image of Rita witnessing the embrace still remains. It is one of the earliest depictions of Rita, probably dating to her own lifetime.

much of life already as a wife, mother and widow; only God knew what awaited her now in the convent. Her great desire to be a nun had been satisfied. That did not mean, however, that everything would go easily for her in religious life. For many years, but especially as a widow, Rita had been accustomed to managing the affairs of her home and allocating her time and resources as she saw fit. Now she would be expected to follow the directives of another. Her days would be scheduled for her. Her freedom and independence would be greatly limited. The nuns, too, realized that, despite her abundant good will and genuine religious spirit, Rita's ability to live this new way of life would have to be tested.

The evidence of the first and most significant test which tradition has carefully handed down to us is preserved not in libraries cataloguing the works of Sister Rita, but in the garden of the convent itself. The community's superior, wishing to assess the new candidate's aptitude for obedience, directed her to water the dead trunk of a barren vine. Rita complied faithfully day after day until finally, to everyone's amazement — especially the superior's — the vine began to flower and then to bear fruit. It continues to do so even today, a living witness to what is possible to those who trust.

For the most part, however, Rita's forty years in the convent were not marked by exceptional events, but by a daily routine of prayer, work and charity. The gentle *Rule* of Saint Augustine around which the community ordered itself, invited the nuns to see everything in their day as a summons to authentic communion of life while together they pursued a deeper intimacy with God. The more Rita grew acquainted with the principles of Augustinian living the more clearly she came to understand what it was that had attracted her to the life of the nuns and friars of Cascia since childhood. In and with those around her she would travel the path to union with Christ. But this would not be a completely new journey for Rita. Only her traveling companions would change. Formerly they had been her parents, spouse and children; now they were the nuns with whom she would share her life for the next forty years.

Saint Mary Magdalene Convent was one of four communities of religious women in Cascia at the time. Another of these was also Augustinian, that of Saint Lucy. A third was Franciscan and the fourth Benedictine. Saint Mary Magdalene had once belonged to the Benedictines as well, but they abandoned it following an earthquake early in the 13th century and the Augustinians subsequently took it over.

The way of life followed by Sister Rita was established by Saint Augustine in the 5th century and articulated in his *Rule*, originally written for his monks, but later adopted by communities of women as well. It is based on the principles for Gospel living practiced by the early Christians of Jerusalem, and recorded in the Acts of the Apostles: love of God and love of neighbor as the chief commandments preached by Jesus, with the sharing of all material possessions in common. By living this core message of Gospel spirituality concretely and faithfully, Augustine believed that he and those who joined with him would form the authentic Church of Jesus — nothing more and nothing less. Saint Augustine personally founded three monastic communities in North Africa but other monks and nuns also adopted his *Rule* for communities which they founded in Africa and throughout the Roman Empire. Thereby the influence of the Bishop of Hippo on monastic life was preserved for posterity even when the African monasteries were destroyed at the very time of Augustine's death.[5]

---

[5] As Augustine lay dying in A.D. 430 at the age of 76, the Vandals were invading North Africa, destroying the Church and dispersing its members. Some who fled to Europe brought Augustine's vision of monastic life with them there, as well as the treasury of his writings and sermons.

By the 12th century many individual monasteries and groups of monastic communities in the various countries of Europe were living according to the *Rule* of Saint Augustine. In 1244 a number of these, principally of Italian origin, were united together to form the Order of Brother Hermits of Saint Augustine, known also and more simply as the Augustinian Order. The Order grew quickly in size, and expanded widely into many towns and cities across the Italian peninsula, responding to the great call for evangelization which the Church was carrying out with new fervor at this time. The friars thus came to Cascia and assumed responsibility for the church of Saint John the Baptist, situated high on the hill in what was then the city's center. Subsequently, with the establishment of two communities of Augustinian Nuns as well, the city of Cascia radiated strongly the spirit of the great African monk and bishop.

A Special Gift

When we consider that Rita's life as an Augustinian religious lasted forty years, it is disappointing that we do not have more information concerning her daily experiences and activities during this quite lengthy period. Yet, the very lack of information

— apart from a few exceptional events — is probably a good indication that life in the convent was rather routine and predictable. Much of the nuns' time was given to the interior life of prayer, contemplation and, for those capable, spiritual reading. At other times they were involved in household tasks, attending to the requests of visitors at the convent door, caring for the poor and disadvantaged who approached them, and quite possibly for some of the nuns at least, visiting the homes of the sick and needy. In general, contact with those outside the convent was limited though, in Sister Rita's time, strict cloister was not observed at Saint Mary Magdalene Convent as it is today.

Certainly the most important and memorable event of Rita's life within the convent was the reception of the thorn of Jesus, which occurred fifteen years before her death. An old and rather credible tradition says that this extraordinary gift was granted Rita on Good Friday in the year 1442. Together with some of the other nuns of the convent, Rita had gone to hear the sermon of the renowned Franciscan, James of the Marches, who had been invited to preach in one of the churches of Cascia on this most solemn day. James was an enthusiastic master of the spoken word who had a special talent for touching the minds and hearts of his audience with vivid imagery and persuasive speech, leading pious souls to a more intense Christian life, and hardened sinners to a true conversion of heart.

On returning to the convent that afternoon Rita went off by herself to pray and was deeply absorbed in adoration before an image of Jesus which was very dear to her: *Jesus of Holy Saturday*, or as it is also known, the *Resurgent Christ*. This depiction of Jesus to which Rita had been devoted long before she entered Saint Mary Magdalene, is so named for its portrayal of the Lord crowned with thorns, showing in his hands and side the wounds of his passion and death, his eyes just beginning to open as the resurrection from the tomb unfolds. As Rita looked upon the suffering Christ whom she had contemplated so many times before, she was moved now by an even deeper awareness of the physical and spiritual burden of pain which he so freely and willingly embraced for love of her and of all humanity. With the tender, compassionate heart of a person fully motivated by grateful love, she spoke her willingness to relieve Christ's suffering by sharing even the smallest part of his pain. Her offer was accepted, her prayer was answered, and Rita was united with Jesus in a profound experience of spiritual intimacy. In this moment of ecstatic union, a thorn from Jesus' crown penetrated Rita's forehead and the wound it caused remained open and visible for the next fifteen years until the day of her death.

Rita was, in fact, one of those individuals we call a stigmatic or stigmatist, but unlike others who have borne visibly the wounds of Jesus in their hands and feet and side, Rita bore only one wound, that caused by the thorn from Jesus' own crown. If the other wounds of Christ were present, but invisible, as has sometimes been the case with other stigmatics, we do not know. What we do know, however, is that the wound of the thorn was truly and fully a sharing in the physical and spiritual suffering of her Lord. Nevertheless, Rita always considered it a very special gift, Jesus' generous response to her own sincere and generous prayer.

Writers and preachers of the past have some-times described Rita's wound as a festering and foul-smelling sore, causing her to become fre-quently isolated from others, even from her fellow religious. While there is no evidence either to confirm or deny this tradition, we do know that the wound did become a serious obstacle for Rita at least once in her lifetime. In the year 1446 Friar Nicholas of Tolentino was to be canonized a saint. As he had been one of Rita's special patrons for much of her life, she wanted very much to join the other nuns who would be making the pilgrimage to Rome for this happy and solemn event. The convent's superior, however, thought that Rita should not go, precisely because of the wound. What a disappointment! But Rita, who was not to be easily dissuaded from her most deeply felt goals, called upon her patron once again for help. The wound healed unexplainably; Rita was able to go to Rome, and on her return to Cascia, it reappeared and remained until her death.

A Sign of Spring

During the last several years of Rita's life a progressively weakened condition kept her confined to bed for long periods of time. It is said that toward the end she was not able to take physical nourishment at all and was sustained on the Eucharist alone. She remained always lucid, however, and shared with the other nuns her great desire to be at last fully united with the Lord whom she had so faithfully sought to follow throughout her life. She was completely at peace and ever thankful to God for the great consolations she had always received from him even during her most difficult challenges.

On one occasion, several months before she died, Rita was visited by a relative from Roccaporena. They talked of many things, calling to mind memories of people and events long gone, still dear to loving hearts. Rita, though a nun for forty years, remained still a faithful wife and mother as well, and as her own earthly pilgrimage was coming to an end, thoughts of those she had loved most in life seemed to fill her conversations and prayers with special tenderness. This visit became a fitting occasion to reminisce. Later that day, before her cousin left the convent, she asked Rita if there was something she might do for her. But Rita needed nothing; she desired nothing. Her heart's only longing was to be one with her Lord. When Rita saw that her cousin was disappointed with her response, she asked her to bring to the convent a rose from the garden of her former home in Roccaporena. Unfortunately the disappointment was not to be lifted. This was the month of January in Cascia high up in the hills of Umbria where winter's snow blanketed the earth and roses were not to be found. Returning home dismayed at her inability to grant Rita's last request, the pensive woman reached the entrance to the village formed by the high rocks that encircled the cluster of houses which was Roccaporena. As she walked the road that led to her home, she passed the house of Rita and Paolo Mancini and, to her astonishment, saw in the snow-covered garden, a single fresh rose on an otherwise dry and barren bush. She immediately returned to the convent where she presented the rose to Rita, who received it with quiet and grateful assurance. Rita understood the rose to be a sign from God. For the four decades she had spent in Cascia's convent she had prayed especially for her husband Paolo, who had died so violently, and for her two sons, who had died so young. The dark, cold earth of Roccaporena, which held their mortal remains, had now produced a beautiful sign of spring and beauty out of season. So, Rita believed, had God brought forth, through her prayers, their eternal life despite tragedy and violence. She now knew that she would soon be one with them again.

Rita died peacefully on May 22, 1457. An old and revered tradition records that the bells of the convent immediately began to peal unaided by human hands, calling the people of Cascia to the doors of the convent, and announcing the triumphant completion of a life faithfully lived. The sorrows and disappointments which had marked Rita's life now passed into history. What remained were the consoling words she heard from her beloved Jesus, "Come, you who are blessed by my Father. Inherit the kingdom prepared for you from the foundation of the world."[6]

---

[6] Matthew 25:34.

The nuns, who had so faithfully cared for Rita throughout her illness, reverently washed and dressed her hallowed body and placed it in the simple wooden coffin, which was the customary final resting place for each of them. Among the people from Cascia and the surrounding territory who came to pay their respects to the convent's most renowned member, was a man by the name of Cicco Barbaro. A carpenter by trade, he had been forced to lay aside his work when he was partially paralyzed as the result of a stroke. As he gazed upon the body of Sister Rita he surely voiced the sentiments of many others as well, when he spoke of the beautiful life of this humble nun and all the good that she had done by bringing lasting peace to the people of Cascia. "If only I were well," he said, "I would have prepared a place more worthy of you." With those heartfelt words he, in fact, was made well. Rita's first miracle was performed. Strength once again returned to Cicco Barbaro's withered arm and hand and, in gratitude, he fashioned the elaborate and richly decorated coffin which would hold Rita's body for several centuries.

The number of people who desired to look upon the gentle face of the "Peacemaker of Cascia" one last time, to touch her hand or to ask her prayers, was so great that Rita's burial had to be delayed. Delayed and delayed, in fact it never took place, for it became clear that something exceptional was occurring. Rather than undergo the ordinary process of decay, it seemed as though this body, once touched by an instrument of Christ's love and passion, was to be free from nature's usual course. It is still preserved today, now in a glass coffin, in the basilica of Cascia.

The coffin built by Cicco Barbaro can still be seen in the convent of Cascia. It is a treasured relic not only for having once held the body of a saint, nor simply for being the grateful work of a man miraculously cured. It is among the oldest artifacts that clearly attest to Rita's spirituality and demonstrates the existence and source of her privileged wound. It also holds the explanation for a long and unhappy tradition concerning her beloved husband, Paolo.

The Long Road

Not surprisingly, devotion to Rita began to spread immediately following her death. Word of the special grace granted to Cicco Barbaro, together with reports of the extraordinary preservation of Rita's body, drew many people to the Convent of Saint Mary Magdalene. A significant number of these, of course, were citizens of Cascia who were personally familiar with Rita; others knew of her through the great gift of peace she brought to the city more than forty years previously. Now, however, still others came to the convent from towns and villages beyond Cascia, either to gaze upon her incorrupt body or in the hope of receiving some favor as Cicco Barbaro had. As they did, they also began to hear the details of Rita's life story from the nuns and townspeople. The faith and courage of Rita, as well as the sufferings and challenges she faced, soon became as captivating to them as the extraordinary details that had first drawn their attention. It was not difficult for many to see in Rita someone very much like themselves, for she had shared the common experience of so many people of that time and place as a spouse and parent, a widow and a consecrated religious. The holiness which her life proclaimed was not of a type distant and foreign to these ordinary Christian faithful. It was reachable and reasonable.

While the reputation of Rita continually brought both the curious and the devout to Saint Mary Magdalene Convent over the years, the formal process of beatification did not begin until more than 150 years after her death. A great promoter of the cause was Costanza Magalotti Barberini, sister-in-law of Pope Urban VIII, himself the former Bishop of Spoleto, the diocese of which Cascia formed a part. On October 26, 1626, Church officials visited the convent, examined the still perfectly incorrupt body, noted the fragrance which emanated from it, inspected the various paintings which depicted the scenes of Rita's life and miracles, interviewed witnesses and recorded testimonies. In all, 51 witnesses were questioned and 76 miraculous occurrences were noted. Four days later, the examiners moved to Roccaporena where they visited Rita's home and garden and viewed the images of her which were preserved there in her native town.

In the following two years Pope Urban issued two documents which would subsequently be accepted as the equivalent of a proper and true decree of beatification. The first was a decree granting to both the Diocese of Spoleto and the Augustinian Order permission to celebrate the liturgical feast of Blessed Rita. The second extended this same privilege to all priests celebrating Mass in any church of the Diocese or in any church throughout the world belonging to the Augustinians.

Finally, on July 16, 1628, a solemn ceremony sealing the long process of beatification took place in the Church of Saint Augustine in Rome, in the presence of Cardinal Antonio Barberini, nephew to Pope Urban, 22 cardinals, and a great number of prelates and faithful. A similar celebration had also been held earlier in the year in Cascia, on the anniversary of Rita's death in the presence of fifteen thousand people. Hereafter Rita was always written and spoken of as "blessed."

Approximately one hundred years later, the then Prior General of the Augustinians gave impetus to the process in the hope of having Rita reach the next and final stage of canonization. Work was resumed in earnest but then suddenly in 1737, without any explanation, everything stopped. Forty years passed and then, in 1775, a nun of Rita's own convent in Cascia, Sister Chiara Isabella Garofali, was suddenly cured through the intercession of Blessed Rita. The alleged miracle was verified through an official diocesan process and the results were sent to the bishop. An examination was then held of Rita's virtues, as well as of four reputed miracles.[7]

On May 24, 1900, Feast of the Ascension of Our Lord, Pope Leo XIII formally proclaimed Rita Lotti, widow of Paolo Mancini, known also as Sister Rita of Cascia, a saint of the Universal Church. He presented her to the world as the "Precious Pearl of Umbria," a model of Christian vir-

---

[7] Four miracles were required because this was the case of a Blessed who had obtained beatification not through the normal procedure but by the approval of her "longstanding cult."

tue and a faithful witness to holiness for the entire People of God. At long last, the name of this little woman of generous heart and unwavering faith became known to Christian people everywhere who were able to recognize in her trials and triumphs, the reality and hope of their own lives as well.

2
Legends

$\mathcal{I}$t was not until many years after her death that the first biography of Rita of Cascia appeared. Remember, she died in 1457 but was not beatified until 1628 and was not canonized until 1900. Long after many of her contemporaries had died, stories circulated which attempted to emphasize the heroic nature of her life and the extraordinary virtue which she practiced. This, coupled with the fact that biographers of long ago were not always as concerned with historical accuracy as they were with inspiring anecdotes and astonishing miracles, explains how so many legends and questionable traditions crept into the story of Saint Rita. Some of these have been mentioned in the preceding text. Others will be mentioned in greater detail here.

Rita's Maligned Spouse

Very often Saint Rita is portrayed as a long-suffering and even abused wife, whose husband was a violent drunkard, and an unfaithful spouse. The tradition behind this story dates far into history and has been repeated almost without variation down to our own time. The fact is that the story is rooted in a tradition now known to be erroneously based, as well as inconsistent with other details of Rita's story.

When Cicco Barbaro miraculously recovered the use of his arm as he prayed before the body of the recently deceased Rita, he set about fashioning a new and solemn casket in which her body was then placed. This casket was decorated inside and out with images depicting Rita, Jesus and Mary Magdalene, as well as with symbols illustrating the spiritual influences on her life. There was also engraved upon its outer cover a poem which spoke of Rita, her suffering and her love. Pilgrims would come to pray before this casket, which was never buried in the ground but remained in a small room within the convent, exposed to the view of visitors. Here they would place devotional candles as signs of their affection and reminders of their prayers. Over many decades the smoke from these candles darkened the casket, eventually making it difficult to read clearly the poetic inscription. In time someone noticed that the poem spoke of a *maritu feroce* or violent husband. Preachers begin to elaborate on this theme, describing Rita's great heroism in patiently enduring the trials and sorrows which her spouse caused her. By the time the first biographies of Rita were written almost a century after her death, the stories of the violent husband had fully developed and have been handed down as one of the major themes of Rita's virtuous life. It was not until the 20th century, when the nuns of Cascia had the monumental casket cleaned and restored, that the *maritu feroce* vanished. It was discovered that the actual wording was *tantu feroce* or *so violent* and the context clearly referred to the fierce wound of Rita's thorn, a suffering of quite a different kind. Old traditions die hard, however, and the stories of Rita's terrible husband continue to be told. This, despite the evidence to the contrary, as well as the great concern of Rita's parents to see her married to a man of their own choosing so that she could be protected from the violence of those turbulent times! We would like to believe that Rita is pleased, however, that her beloved spouse's reputation is slowly being restored.

The Miraculous Bees

There are two stories concerning bees that are told in connection with Saint Rita. The first, which concerns her infancy, has already been mentioned. The second, quite distinct from the first, records the existence of white bees in one of the exterior walls of the convent, not far from the place where the miraculous vine still grows. These bees only began to appear long after Rita's death. They are bees without stingers, said to exist in only two places in the world. Their connection with Saint Rita is only indirect: they have taken up residence where she lived and died. Curious, however, is the fact that the coat of arms of the Barberini family, mentioned above in relation to Saint Rita's beatification, contains bees.

The Miracle of the Figs

This story is often told in connection with the miracle of the rose and, in fact, is said to have followed upon it. After the same cousin who had discovered the beautiful, scented flower in the snow-covered garden brought it to Rita, the nun then asked for two figs. The relative, this time certain that she would be able to grant the request, returned to Roccaporena, picked the figs from the frozen tree, and returned with them to Cascia. Some see in the combined images of the rose and two figs symbols of Rita's husband and two sons.

3

Disciple and Patron

Mother Teresa Fasce

In the port city of Genoa, in northern Italy, a young woman entered the Augustinian Church of Our Lady of Consolation for the devotions honoring the Church's newest canonized saint. As she listened to the story of Rita's life, of her great hardships but even greater love, this woman's own attraction for religious life was inflamed. The words of the preacher touched her heart and confirmed her desire to follow the example of the Augustinian Nun. Hardly could she imagine at the time, however, the many ways in which her path would resemble that of this new saint.

Maria Giovanna Fasce was nineteen years old in 1900. She had been born into a large and comfortable family on December 27, 1881. As a young girl she had been afforded the opportunity of an education and the future seemed promising for her. She had considered religious life before but now felt absolutely certain that this was the path she was to follow. While her family had no objection to Maria's vocational choice, they could not comprehend, nor accept, her desire to embrace this vocation in faraway Cascia, then a tiny, impoverished and backward hamlet of central Italy. Not even

Rita's canonization had done much to improve the quality of life of the town or of the convent there, both reduced to insignificance caused by earthquakes which had ravished the area several times over since Rita's death. Why must she go to Cascia? Why not one of the Augustinian convents nearer to home in northern Italy? "God wants me in Cascia," was Maria's firm response to every question and protest. The family finally relented, only to have another and more formidable difficulty arise. The nuns themselves refused her request to join them, just as centuries earlier Rita's own initial petition for admission had been denied. The Abbess judged, wisely it might seem by today's standards, that a young girl raised in a large, modern city like Genoa, exposed to many opportunities and a good education, would find it much too difficult to adjust to the simple and difficult life of Cascia. Surprised and saddened, Maria held her ground and resolved never to leave her hometown unless it was to go to Cascia. Fortunately one of the friars of Consolation Church in Genoa, Father Mariano Ferriello, Maria's confessor, took up her cause and petitioned the nuns on her behalf. Finally, the desired response came, and Maria was told to come.

Maria arrived in Cascia on June 20, 1906 and two days later, on the Feast of the Sacred Heart, was admitted to the convent. She was a postulant for six months until Christmas night when she received the Augustinian habit and began her novitiate. Again on Christmas night of the following year, 1907, Maria made her profession of vows, taking the name Sister Maria Teresa Eletta. While there was much in these first years of religious life following profession that brought her great joy and consolation, there were not lacking difficulties and trials as well that caused her considerable dismay. On the advice of her former confessor, Father Mariano, Sister Maria Teresa requested a period of exclaustration from the convent so that she could return home and consider well the path the Lord wanted her to follow. In June, 1910, Sister Maria Teresa left Cascia and returned to Genoa where she spent the next eleven months with her family, living faithfully, nonetheless, all of the demands of her religious profession. Finally, her questions and doubts having been resolved, she returned to the convent in May 1911 and the following March 22nd, made her solemn profession with great conviction and resolve. In 1914, Sister Maria Teresa was appointed Mistress of Novices and in 1917 was named Vicar, or assistant to the Abbess. Her life of virtue, marked especially by her great humility and devotion to all the expectations of religious life, did not go unnoticed by her sisters. On August 12, 1920 she was elected Abbess by the unanimous vote of the community and, over the next twenty-seven years until her death, was re-elected unanimously nine times.

Mother Maria Teresa's program as Abbess was one of enriching and deepening the religious spirit of the convent and its members. This she accomplished not by rules or demands but by her own example, gentleness and personal concern for each of the nuns. Under her guidance and leadership the community steadily grew in size as well as in religious spirit. The influence which she exercised was felt not only within the convent walls, but in Cascia and throughout the world as well. Mother, as she was simply and affectionately known by all, established an orphanage attached to the convent to care for young girls, built a seminary for the training of Augustinian Friars and a hospital for the people of the town. She initiated a magazine to promote devotion to Saint Rita and set plans for the building of a large church to be dedicated to the saint and to minister to the increasing numbers of pilgrims coming to Cascia. These many projects were all carried out by a cloistered, contemplative nun who was zealous in living her spiritual life and who was continuously burdened by physical ailments. Shortly after she was first elected Abbess, Mother was operated on to remove a tumor from her breast. Eight years later she underwent a second operation for the same malady. But breast cancer was not her only illness. She suffered also from heart sickness, asthma, diabetes and severe circulatory problems which caused excruciating pain in her feet. In all of this suffering Mother was never heard to complain and was apologetic that her ailments caused inconveniences to the other sisters who, however, never considered any of these a burden.

On Saturday, January 18, 1947 Mother Maria Teresa died serenely despite her great suffering. Initially entombed in the local cemetery of Cascia, her body was transferred later in the year to the lower crypt of the basilica whose completion that May she had not lived to see. Soon after, the cause of Mother's canonization was begun, and on October 12, 1997, she was beatified by Pope John Paul II. Mother's incorrupt body now rests in a new glass coffin not far from the saint she so loved and sought to imitate.

4

Devotion and Devotions

*W*ith the canonization of Saint Rita in 1900, interest in and devotion to the "Precious Pearl of Umbria" spread rapidly not only in her native Italy, but throughout many nations. Though she was not a saint of the modern world, she certainly became a saint for modern times. As a woman who had experienced the various states of life as wife and widow, mother and nun, Rita had much to say to women of every time and place. As a victim of violence and a witness to forgiveness, she offered powerful testimony to men and women both. Devotion to Saint Rita, which blossomed in the United States in the first decades of the 20th century, was centered around two shrine churches established by the Augustinians under the patronage of their religious sister, one in Chicago and one in Philadelphia. In the latter city, where the National Shrine of Saint Rita was established in 1907, there has been a striking resurgence of interest in the little woman of Cascia. Perhaps the words of Pope John Paul II, on the occasion of the centenary of Rita's canonization during the Holy Year 2000, explain the reason:

"In her example of total surrender to God, in her transparent simplicity and in her steadfast fidelity to the Gospel, it is possible for us, too, to find the appropriate indication of how we are to be true Christians at the dawn of this third millennium. What is the message which this saint gives us? It is a message which comes from her life: humility and obedience were the path along which Rita walked toward an ever more perfect union with the Crucified. The stigma which shines on her forehead is the proof of her Christian maturity. On the cross with Jesus, she has, in a certain sense, "obtained her degree" in that love which she had already known and expressed in an heroic way within the walls of her home and in her participation in the affairs of her village.... Today, 100 years after her canonization, I would like to present her once again, as a sign of hope, especially to families. Dear families, imitating her example, you too will learn how to find, in attachment to Christ, the strength needed to bring to fulfillment your mission in the service of the culture of love."[8]

---

[8] Address of Pope John Paul II, 20 May 2000, in St. Peter's Square. *L'Osservatore Romano*, 21 May 2000.

Saint Rita, Peacemaker

Devotion to Saint Rita under the title "peace-maker" is readily understandable to those familiar with her life and the challenges she always met with courage and faith. Her life with the Lord Jesus filled her with peace, which is the gift promised to those who seek God's will despite hardship and disappointment. This gift which Rita received she freely shared, becoming a channel of God's peace and an instrument of reconciliation for others. In a world that knows so well the divisions and conflicts which touch families, neighbors, societies and nations, devotion to Saint Rita, the Peace-maker, is both timely and appealing.

Saint of the Impossible

Tradition says that this title, which Saint Rita shares with Saint Jude, was first given to her by her many devotees in Spain. Though the title's history may be obscure, the basis for it is not. In her own life there was much that was difficult, much that may have seemed impossible to deal with: the frustration of her plans, the murder of her spouse, the obstinacy and death of her children. Any of these might have turned her against God or made her a bitter woman. But such was not the case. Instead, every difficulty and trial drew her more closely to her God in whom, she was firmly convinced, all things were possible. With faith and grace Rita overcame every difficulty. Nothing was impossible for her. A second explanation for the title is offered in consideration of the numerous miracles that have been attributed to Saint Rita's intercession, many of them truly difficult and even hopeless situations. For some she is the saint of final appeal.

A Saint Who Asks Too Much?

In some circles it is said that Saint Rita is one who always asks a high price for any favor she grants. Whenever she gives something, it is reported, she takes something away. It would seem that this story has been circulated not by Rita's friends but by her enemies. Indeed, there is a sense, however, in which something is taken away when a favor is granted: fear is taken away, or suffering or sickness or hardness of heart. But who would not desire to be rid of any of these? No, Saint Rita is not a demanding saint in this respect. So many have recourse to her, so many speak of favors received through her friendship. So many find her fully the compassionate and tender woman her story reveals her to be.

Postscript

When the General Calendar of the Latin Rite was revised following the reform of the Second Vatican Council, Saint Rita was one of the saints whose memorial was not included on the new calendar. The understanding among Augustinians is that this occurred, at least in part, because reliably historical data on Saint Rita's life was very scant. Shortly thereafter, the nuns of Saint Rita Monastery in Cascia asked Fr. Damasus Trapp, OSA, an historian and former Postulator General of the Order, to do research into the life and times of Saint Rita. The results of his work were published in four volumes between the years 1968 and 1970, under the title *Documentazione Ritiana Antica*. Father Trapp's monumental work is a significant source for the material found in this book. The writings of two other Augustinians have been consulted as well: "Santa Rita. Estudio historico critico sobre sus primeras biografias y sobre su vida," published in the journal *Archivo Agustiniano* 73 (1989) by Fr. Balbino Rano, OSA, and *The Message of Saint Rita of Cascia*, by Fr. Agostino Trape, OSA, published by Augustinian Press, Villanova in 1989.

Other sources include:

Blessed Maria Teresa Fasce, by M. Papalini, 1997.
Rita of Cascia, Priceless Pearl of Umbria, by V. Perri, 1995.
Santa Rita da Cascia, Storia, Devozione, Sociologia, Institutum Historicum Augustinianum, 2000.

Finally, it is a joy to be able to note that the most recent publication of the *Missale Romanum*, released to the press on March 25, 2002, has once again placed on the Universal Calendar the feast of Saint Rita of Cascia, religious, under the date of 22 May.

ST PAULS

This book was produced by St. Pauls/Alba House, the Society of St. Paul, an international religious congregation of priests and brothers dedicated to serving the Church through the communications media.

For information regarding this and associated ministries of the Pauline Family of Congregations, write to the Vocation Director, Society of St. Paul, P.O. Box 189, 9531 Akron-Canfield Road, Canfield, Ohio 44406-0189. Phone (330) 702-0359; or E-mail: spvocationoffice@aol.com or check our internet site, www.albahouse.org